kate

the
kate moss
book

kate
the
kate moss
book

by Kate Moss with a foreword by Liz Tilberis   Universe Publishing

First published in the United States of America in 1995
by UNIVERSE PUBLISHING
A Division of Rizzoli International Publications, Inc.
300 Park Avenue South
New York, NY 10010

Designed by Phil Bicker
Production Jessica Hallett

95 96 97 98 99 / 10 9 8 7 6 5 4 3 2 1

Printed and bound in Italy

Library of Congress Catalog Card Number 95-60245

Following pages: Juergen Teller, New York, June 1994

To Mum & Dad

1 in the beginning 2 5'6" the breakthrough 3 for fun no

oney 4 obsession 5 make-up and hairdo's 6 and so it goes

David Ross
1990
Unpublished

This book is the story, told in pictures, of how one remarkable
English girl became one of the great fashion legends of the
nineties. When Kate Moss came to see us at *Harper's Bazaar* in
New York 1992, she had already worked, mostly for *The Face*, in
London. The second she walked into our office, model editor Sara
Foley and Fashion Director Paul Cavaco knew they were looking at
a true beauty; someone whose face and attitude were a
personification of the time. There was just one problem: Kate
was small. When she stood up against our office wall, she
measured a shade less than 5'7". Still, *Bazaar's* editors
figured, small models had succeeded in the past (though they
were exceptional) – and this girl was so mesmerizing, she was
worth a try. The result was a nine-page story in *Bazaar's*
relaunch issue, September 1992. From that point onward, there
was no stopping Kate. She signed a contract with Calvin Klein,
and her image was projected, through the extraordinary power of
his advertising, around the world, on bus shelters, billboards,
TV and magazines. Meanwhile, she became a runaway star – more
than holding her own against the army of 5'10"-plus girls she
was sharing the catwalk with.

   Harper's Bazaar has continued to use Kate Moss ever since –
many of the photographs that appear in this book originated in
our magazine – because, above all, she's a great model. That is
to say, Kate is highly adaptable, looks good in a lot of make-up,
and in no make-up at all, is easy to work with and puts
everything into her job. All those qualities have given her the
instinct to move on when fashion changes, so she has never been
trapped by labels. Calvin Klein, too, has been impressed by her
range, which he defines as 'Very sexy and beautiful and
glamorous and appealing'. Even surrounded by a huge media
furore, Kate has always stayed cool. What she has achieved is
remarkable for a twenty-one-year-old. Congratulations, Kate.

Liz Tilberis, Editor-in-Chief, *Harper's Bazaar*, January 1995

When I was approached with the idea of doing a book, I
was at first apprehensive for a number of reasons. One
being that it felt almost like a retrospective, which
made me feel very uncomfortable. That is to say, a
retrospective of my work at the age of twenty is, in my
opinion, just slightly premature. I was adamantly
against it. They (the infamous they) would not give up,
the more I was pursued, the more I was forced to think
of a different approach for the book. On the one hand I
didn't want to do it because it did feel like a
retrospective, and on the other, that was THE reason to
do it. It is a retrospective, not necessarily of my
work, but of six years of fashion, and the work of some
of the greatest photographers, make-up artists,
hairdressers and stylists in the business.

To say this book is about me (which is the MAIN reason
I was uncomfortable - me, me, me, me, me...
Frightening!) is ridiculous. This book is not about me.
It is more about all the people I have been lucky enough
to work with. It is impossible for me to thank them
properly for the opportunity, not only to have worked
with them, and to have been a part of their vision, but
also, for selflessly allowing their images to appear in
this book. I thank them beyond words.

To me this book is a celebration of the photographers,
of change, and of growth.

I feel blessed to have come as far as I have come. I was discovered on an airplane by a woman named Sarah Doukas, at the age of fourteen. I don't know why that happened. I don't know why any of this happened. The chain of events that followed has led me to where I am now, and I wouldn't attempt to question any of it, or ask why. It's none of my business.

I only know that at the age of twenty, I have travelled all over the world and have seen and learned about many different cultures, an education that is not available at any school. I consider myself extremely lucky. I also realize that with any amount of good, comes a certain amount of bad. That's fine. A lot of horrible, unfair, untrue things have been said about me. I've been labelled viciously by the majority of the media, which in turned has fuelled the rumour mill. The things said about me have been so ludicrous, that I have never given them enough credence to retaliate.

I can only say that the best revenge is success. And that the more visible they make me, the more invisible I become.

love Kate x

Kate Moss
Aspen, December 1994

PS. I am just on my way out to dinner, to eat a massive steak and loads of very fattening potatoes, with loads of butter. KM

in the beginning

*Opposite and
following pages:*
Corinne Day
London, 1989

KODAK TMX 5052

22

Corinne Day
May 1990
for *The Face*

Corinne Day
July 1990
The Third Summer of Love
for *The Face*

Above and following pages:
Alex Szaszy
1990
Footage from the Third Summer of Love

Previous pages
and this page:
Robert Scott
London, 1990
Unpublished

Owen Scarbiena
1990
Unpublished

Lewis Mulatero
London, August 1990

David Sims
London, 1990

5'6" the breakthrough

Manuela Pavesi
1992
for Italian *Glamour*

Manuela Pavesi
Paris, 1992
for Italian *Glamour*

Ellen von Unwerth
New York, 1992
Unpublished

Following pages:
Juergen Teller
Katharine Hamnett campaign
1992

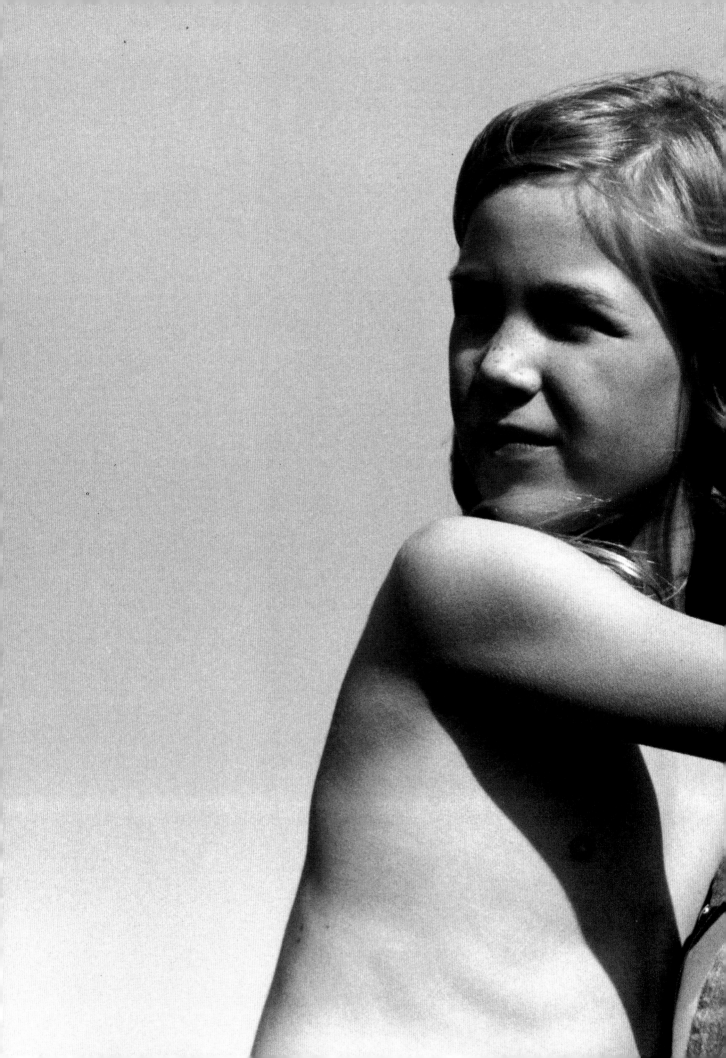

Mario Sorrenti
London, September 1992
for *The Face*

Mario Sorrenti
London, February 1993
for British *Elle*

Enrique Badulescu
May 1992
for *The Face*

Corinne Day
London, 1992
Unpublished

Ian Thomas
Spain, 1992
Unpublished

Patrick Demarchelier
New York, September 1992
for *Harper's Bazaar*

Sante D'Orazio
New York, 1992
for *Allure*

Following pages:
Helmut Newton
Paris, November 1992
for *Yves Saint Laurent*
Rive Gauche Campaign

Steven Meisel
for Dolce & Gabbana, 1992-3
catalogue

for fun not money

Opposite and
following pages:
Mario Sorrenti
Virgin Gorda, 1992

Arthur Elgort
Nepal, December 1993

Mario Sorrenti
Virgin Gorda, 1992

obsession

Patrick Demarchelier
1994
for *Calvin Klein*

This page:
Patrick Demarchelier

Opposite page:
Patrick Demarchelier
Tiziano Magni
Mario Sorrenti
November 1993
for *Calvin Klein*

Previous pages
and this page:
David Sims
New York,1993
for *Calvin Klein*

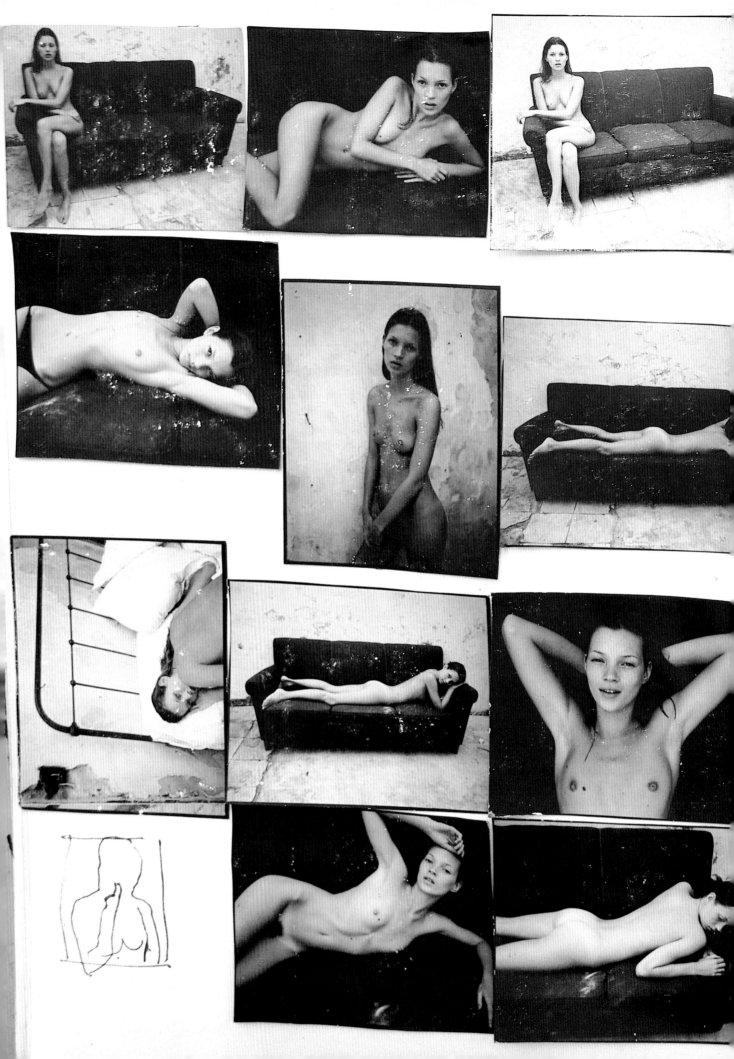

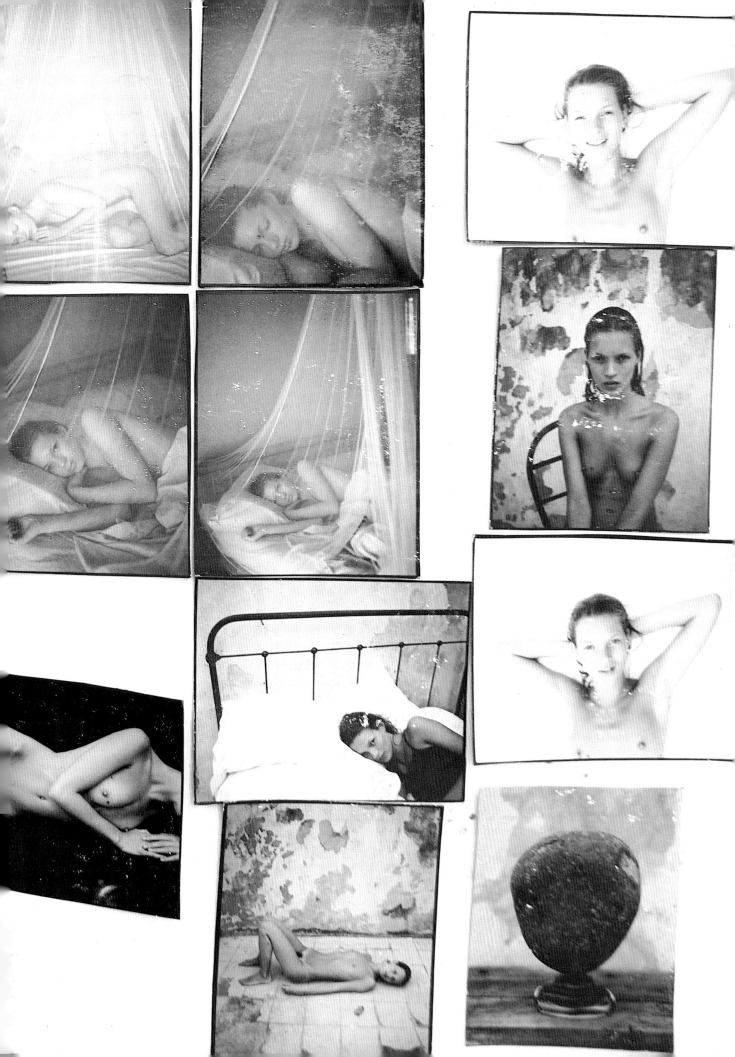

Steven Meisel
New York City, May 1994
for Calvin Klein

make-up and hairdo's

Corinne Day
1993
for British *Vogue*

Paolo Rovorci
January 1994
for French *Vogue*

Patrick Demarchelier
St Barts French West Indies
April 1994
for *Harper's Bazaar*

David Sims
New York City, December 1993
for *Harper's Bazaar*

Opposite and previous pages:
Mario Sorrenti
1992
for *Harper's Bazaar*

Thiery Le Goues
Paris, October 1993
for English *Esquire*

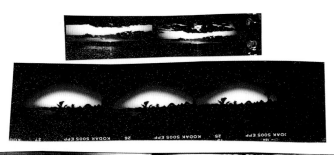

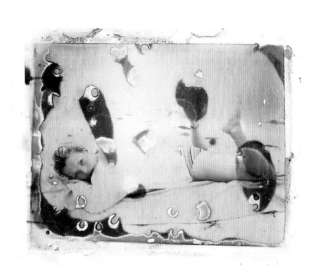

Previous pages and this page:
Enrique Badulescu
Mexico, January 1994
for *Harper's Bazaar*

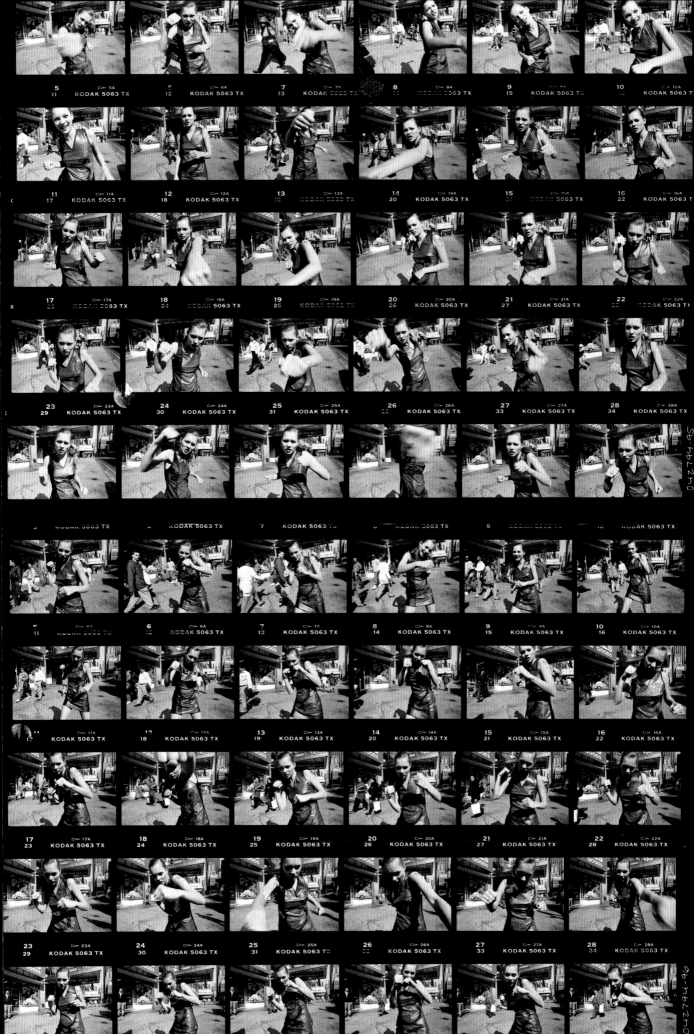

Peter Lindbergh
Rome, June 1994
for *Harper's Bazaar*

Steven Klein
New York, January 1994
for *Mademoiselle*

Following pages:
Juergen Teller
Paris, April 1994
for American *Vogue*

and so it goes

Juergen Teller
New York City, September 1994
for American *Vogue*

This page and previous pages:
Juergen Teller
London, April 1994
for German *Harper's Bazaar*

Following pages:
Ellen von Unwerth
September 1994
for American *Vogue*

Nick Knight
London, December 1994
for British *Vogue*

This page and following pages:
Glen Luchford
New York City, April 1994
for *Harper's Bazaar*

kent mogg

Polaroids:
Various
Main pictures:
Roxanne Lowit

Juergen Teller
New York, 1994
Unpublished

MOSS TELLS AL
P DOGGY DOGG
LM McLAREN•PULP
T LANG•TIM ROTH
TURN OF THE SUIT

WHAT D...
WOMEN WANT?
Eternal youth
and HRT (whatever the risks)

Kate Moss
photographed by
Michael Roberts

HEAVEN
ON EARTH
Vicki Woods adrift in the Seychel...
John Hatt on the hamster tra... Syria
PLUS ...rgio Armani, Charlotte Lewis,
...itoraj and Kingsley Amis

ZOO TV
The Word, The Big Breakfast:
the future of television?

VOGUE

VOGUE
MAR
£2.50

MOVE INTO
SPRING...
The colours
the layers
the freedom
that make
the difference

Sex, drugs and science:
their future together

SHOULD WOMEN DIE
FOR THEIR COUNTRY?

LONDON STYLE...
LONDON GIRLS

fashion's
new spirit

THE FACE

No 22 JULY 1990 £1.50 • US $4.75

THE 3RD
SUMMER
OF LOVE

Stone Roses on
Spike Island,
an A-Z of the
new bands, Daisy
Age fashion,
Hendrix and
psychedelia

'Kiss my butt'
Sandra on
Madonna

Prince in
Minneapolis:
tour preview

JOHN WATERS / MICKEY ROURKE / MARSHALL JEFFERSON / TIM ROTH

BAZAAR
Harper's

Perfection!

GLAMOUR

OCTOBRE 16 F

KATE
MOSS
TOP MODEL
Comment la petite
est devenue grande

MODE
Peace and love

McCARTNEY
Un entretien
domestique

INTERVIEW
Isabelle Huppert
par Bob Wilson

20 OU 40 ANS
La beauté sans rides

PSY
Sommes-nous toutes
...es ?

COMAGE 2.50
FRENCH GLAMOUR

GUIDE
Le Sienne
de Liane
Foly

GLAMOUR

ROCKA
BILLY

l'oriente
a Parigi
i ribelli
USA

moda e beauty:
è romantico.

BAZAAR
Harper's

fashion's
Movement
to Is
ing?

...uly's
...Debate

ELLE

numéro
anglo
di...

ondres!

Harpers
OCTOBER 1993

£2.50

& per

Contributing photographers:

ENRIQUE BADULESCU

NEIL DAVENPORT

CORINNE DAY

PATRICK DEMARCHELIER

SANTE D'ORAZIO

ARTHUR ELGORT

MARK HISPARD

STEVEN KLEIN

NICK KNIGHT

MARK LE BON

THIERY LE GOUES

PETER LINDBERGH

ROXANNE LOWIT

GLEN LUCHFORD

STEVEN MEISEL

LEWIS MULATERO

HELMUT NEWTON

MANUELA PAVESI

DAVID ROSS

PAOLO ROVERSI

OWEN SCARBIENA

ROBERT SCOTT

DAVID SIMS

MARIO SORRENTI

ALEX SZASZY

JUERGEN TELLER

IAN THOMAS

CHRISTY TURLINGTON

ELLEN VON UNWERTH

ALBERT WATSON

So this is one of the most beautiful women in world

THE LANGUAGE OF INFLUENCE

CASUAL: Kate Moss at Heathrow Picture: DENNIS STONE

That's torn it, Kate

SHE could be a student thumbing a lift up the M1 in her torn leggings and tattered trainers, carrying an old plastic bag.

But there is little need to put on appearances when you are one of the most beautiful women in the world, jetting off for an international modelling assignment.

Kate Moss flew out to New York from Heathrow yesterday to model for Vogue magazine. And fellow passengers could only stare at the casually-attired queen of the catwalk.

Kate, 19, became a superstar overnight after appearing in Vogue earlier this year.

Pictures of the waif-like model clad in sexy underwear were branded obscene by some irate readers.

Now she is usually seen wearing glamorous designer clothes. But not, apparently, when she is off-duty.

The superwaif off duty: 'I want to find something I really love, because I don't love modelling. Fashion's not satisfying at all. You can't change the world through fashion'   *Photograph: Glynn Griffiths*

She's still only 19, a gauche teenager, and is endearingly polite. It's enough to restore your faith in supermodels

Kate Moss asks if she can have a fag

LOVE

29 USA

Kate Moss
c\o Men/Women
107 Green St., 2nd Floor
New York, NY 10012

2/94

ОБОЗРЕВАТЕЛЬ

Кейт Мосс:
царевна-
лягушка
XXI века

Many thanks to: Linda Moss, Peter Moss and Nick Moss, Paul Cavaco, Sara Foley, Derek Golomka, Fabien Baron and Liz Tilberis at *Harper's Bazaar*, Calvin Klein, Lyn Tesoro, Trish Becker, Carolyn Bessete, David A Lowrie, Neil Kraft and all at Calvin Klein, Mimi Brown at Art and Commerce NYC, Kim Sion, Scott Kraenzlein, Tara Turner at Smile Management, Julie Brown and Victoria Sullivan at Map, Chris Schramm and Marion Debeaupre, Patricia McMahon, Missy Mixon and Phoebe Houghton at Z Photographic, Katy Baggot and Charlotte Wheeler, Michelle Ocampo, Jung Vhoi, Tomo Delaney at British *Elle*, Eric Blanpied, Roberto and Vanessa at Studio Roberto, Xandra, Robin Derrick, Lucinda Chambers and all at British *Vogue*, Linda Cantello, Kevin Aucoin, François Nars, Dick Page, Miranda Joyce, Lucia Pieroni, Mary Greenwell, Kay Montano, Sam McKnight, James Brown, Julien Dy's, Drew Jarrett, Venetia Scott, Melanie Ward, Danilo, Orlando, Scassia Gambaccini, Grace Coddington, Brahne Wolfe, Camilla Nickerson, Roxanne Lowit, Isobel Givan, Diana Edkins and all at American *Vogue*, Sarah Doukas, Simon Chambers, Jackie Powell and all at Storm Model Management, Paul Rowland, Jennifer Ramey, Stuart Cameron, John Gnerre and all at Women Model Management, David Brown at Riccardo Gay, Guido, Johnny Depp, Anke, Polly Hamilton, Barbara Pfister, Jessica Hallett, Polly Mellen, Wendell Maruyama, Phil Bicker, John Critchley, Daren Ellis, Jake Chessum, John Akehurst, JB, John Spinks and anyone else that I have worked with or has helped me that I have not been able to name here.

Major thanks to all of the contributors and photographers without whom this book could not have been made: Enrique Badulescu, Neil Davenport, Corinne Day, Patrick Demarchelier, Sante D'Orazio, Arthur Elgort, Mark Hispard, Steven Klein, Nick Knight, Mark Le Bon, Thiery Le Goues, Peter Lindbergh, Roxanne Lowit, Glen Luchford, Steven Meisel Lewis Mulatero, Helmut Newton, Manuela Pavesi, David Ross, Paolo Roversi, Owen Scarbiena, Robert Scott, David Sims, Mario Sorrenti, Alex Szaszy, Juergen Teller, Ian Thomas, Christy Turlington, Ellen von Unwerth and Albert Watson.

In loving memory of Ian Thomas   Kate